MILLION STARS

CHANGING LIVES,
FINDING FREEDOM, AND
BUILDING PERSONAL POWER

Alexis
you're a joy &
An inspiration!!!
♡ Fatima

FATIMA OMAR KHAMISSA

Typesetting and formatting by access ideas

ISBN: 978-0-9953136-3-7

CONTENTS

Forward

What Does Leadership Look Like?

Leadership roles are all around us. There is political leadership through Prime Ministers, Presidents, Queens and Kings. There is community leadership through Imams, Clerics and Rabbis. There is business leadership your employees, employers, managers and bosses. There is family leadership within your homes through being a parent, sister, or brother. There is also leadership when it comes to the role that you, yourself, play in life.

Now you might be thinking, *"Why are you talking about leadership? Where does leadership start? What does it look like? How does it show up in the world?"*

When you take a look at all the events occurring around the world today, it is easy for us to label things as good or bad, and right or wrong. When you see all the bad happening in the world it makes you feel like you can't do anything about it. You often find yourself saying, "I can't change the world. I can't make a difference. I am so small compared to this massive world and the number of people in it."

The truth is that you *can* make a difference. Leadership is not telling other people what to do; rather, it is guiding others towards a goal.

I want you to imagine that you went to a movie or a live theater performance and the entire stage was set. The loud audience, the producers, the cast and the characters are all present. A large amount of money was spent to make the set absolutely perfect. Everything is in order, and everyone is awaiting the arrival of the main star of the show.

The star of the show is you.

You arrived! It's the day you were born! You have arrived! They place you into your little cot, and the stage is set. All of your limiting beliefs, all of the programs, all the people, all the cast members, your grandparents, your uncles, your aunties, your cousins, and everybody was waiting for the star to arrive. You are the star in your show and everyone else plays a part in that.

You are the sum total of all your experiences. Where you were born, what you were taught, who you looked up to as a role model, the school you went to, the people you were surrounded by; all of your experiences influence what leadership looks like to you.

The beginning of leadership is you, standing on your own feet, and taking responsibility for yourself as your word and your promise. Do you say what you mean and do you mean what you say? Who are you? Are you a liar? Do you say something and then do another thing? Can I trust you when you say something? Or are all of your words filled with deceit? Are you a hard worker? Are you the funny one? Are you the good looking one? What labels were put on you? Are you still living a life with those old labels?

It's time to take another look at your labels and the roles that you play. It's time to look with different glasses.

Everything that is going on in the world, is going on inside of you. Whatever is messed up in the world, is messed up in you. You are a small portion of the world and it's inside of you. You represent the world and the world represents you. If the world is at war, you are at war. If the world is racist, you are racist. If the world is unjust, you are unjust. You are a direct reflection of the world. Every time you label someone and you call them a word and you say, "You are a liar" or "You're an idiot", you are actually labeling yourself.

It is time for us to stand up and take our place in the sun. It is time for us to be leaders! It is time for us to step into our authenticity and restore our integrity. You have been playing small. You think the world is going to be just fine because you don't play a role in it, but, you are the world and you are in it.

To be a leader is to be kind. To be a leader is to be generous. To be a leader is to be compassionate. To be a leader is to step into your truth. To be a leader is to stop the racism and accept everybody for who they are. To be a leader is to open your arms and welcome people even if they are flawed.

Leadership is for you to stand up and say, *"What is that one small thing that I can do today in my home, in my community, in my mosque, in my neighbourhood, in my church, in my synagogue that will be an act of love and mercy?"*

What if all your beautiful acts of compassion and kindness were done, without expecting anything in return?

You are never too old or too young to take on the role of a leader. You often underestimate children and their ability to be leaders at a young age. However, a child can take on the role of a leader by starting at home. Even if it is something as small as being in charge of watering the plants, or taking out the garbage, or setting the table. Allow your children to take on something extraordinary and watch how they surprise you.

Leadership starts at home. The question is, how are you raising leaders in your house? For me, from the time a child is born, they are a leader. That's the new leader that I'm raising. I'm raising this child to become the president of their school, to become an honor roll student, to become the new Prime Minister. I'm raising this person to become a doctor, a lawyer, an accountant.

How do you create a leader if I'm not the leader? How do you create leaders if you're a follower? How do you create a leader if you're a victim? How do you create a leader if you have this "need to be needed"? How do you raise a leader if you "need to be in control" all the time? The answer is; you don't.

Who you raise is who you are.

When you look at your children and you look at the qualities in your children; that is who you are. They represent you and your family. Your children and their actions represent you and your family, and that is what leadership is all about. Leadership is you being the leader; you embodying the behavior, not you telling other people what to do. You have to be the leader to help others. You have to be the leader to train your children.

A leader is kind, a leader is compassionate, and a leader is gentle, yet firm.

There are two types of leaders; charismatic and transformational. A charismatic leader is one who influences their followers with the use of their personality and charm. A transformational leader is one who owns their leadership. They inspire change through their vision and passion. Transformational leaders is what our society needs now.

Your experiences influence what you consider leadership to be. You can make a difference in the world. Take action to become a transformational leader and share your passion, goals and vision with those around you. No one is born a leader, but anyone can become a great one!

Love, Fatima

November 14, 2017

Introduction

I imagine a world where women are free. Free to own property, claim inheritance, have our own bank accounts, and travel by ourselves. A world were women are CEO's of companies, master coaches, world-class leaders and international speakers - you can do all of this and have thriving families too. A world where women are safe, independent, make healthy choices about their bodies, and be connected to their creator. This is the time when women can absolutely have it all! The best of the best!

Million Stars Academy was created to help women regardless of race, religion, faith, ethnicity, and cultural background. No matter what your history is, or what you've gone through in the past, I want you to be able to make a difference in your communities, villages, cities and countries. I want to empower you wherever you are in life, so that you can make money and have choices. My job as a leader, is to create, teach, and train other leaders. If you're reading this right now, that is who you are! I'm happy to meet you and welcome you to the Million Stars journey. You're absolutely going to love it!

CHAPTER 1

Red Dot

In this chapter, you are going to participate in my famous "red dot exercise" and If you've ever been to an airport or shopping center and gotten lost, you may have found yourself needing to find the information desk or map.

On the map, there is a red dot that says "YOU ARE HERE." In this exercise, you simply want to know where you are right now. Once you know where you are, you can find out where you are going next. Without judging yourself, simply write down where you are in life. Be truthful; as if you were in a courtroom speaking the truth and nothing but the truth.

Grab a pen and paper

No judgement. No opinions. Think about where you are in business, money, confidence level, and relationships. Where are you in your significant relationships? Where are you in relationship to your body? Education? Are you happy with your life, your home, your neighborhood? Get present in your life. Do you want to volunteer more? Exercise more? This exercise should make you conscious of where you are right now. Be present.

Notes: ✍

CHAPTER 2

Are You Designed for Greatness?

Each and every human being is going through pain. Whether it is spiritual pain, emotional pain, physical pain etc. The presence of some kind of pain is always going to be there. Perhaps you got lied to, or cheated on, or divorced, or robbed; the pain is always there.

You might be asking yourself, "*Why are you talking about greatness when I have so much pain? Why are you asking me am I designed for greatness? What has that got to do with my pain?*" When it comes to pain, you have two choices; jump right into it and choose to struggle and suffer with all the stories related to that pain, or you can step into your greatness by using the pain for your purpose.

A situation occurred with my sister who lives in South Africa, where three robbers came into the house. She was in the house with her husband and their four children under the age of 14. The thieves came into the house, shot my brother-in-law three times and stabbed him. Luckily, neither the bullet, nor the knife touched any of his major organs. He was placed in ICU and, after a few days, he was sent home.

However, the trauma and pain that my brother-in-law, my sister and the children went through will stay with them forever. Imagine the children waking up in the middle of the night to see their father being assaulted. One of the robbers grabbed my sister and put a gun to her head. Thankfully, they didn't touch her because my brother-in-law was shouting and telling them, "Leave her alone." She went back into the bedroom, locked her door and immediately began calling friends and family for help

When I found out about what had happened, I was terrified and felt a rush of emotions begin to take over. In that moment, I asked myself; *"How do I find my greatness?"* I'm all the way in Canada, she's all the way in South Africa. I can't go over there and hold my sister or comfort her, and be there for the children. Because I live in Canada.

How do I step into my greatness in this situation?

When you find yourself in a situation where you are suffering with pain, there are three things that will assist you to step into your greatness; control your tongue, don't go into the negativity of that pain, and keep on reaching for your God.

Out of all three, the last one is the most important one. Keep on reaching for your Creator and gain closeness to Him in every kind of calamity, trials and adversity. Give charity, do the good things that God wants you to do. The truth is; bad things are going to happen even to good people. This life is a life of trials and tests, so keep your eyes on the prize.

So, the question is; are you designed for greatness? Yes, you are! You were made for greatness. You have been created to be great in all ways possible and every single one of you has that greatness inside of us. It doesn't matter what happens in your life; you are not a victim. Being a victim is a choice that you make.

Going back to what happened to my sister, let's break it down completely. What really happened? What happened was: three robbers came into the house and held them up at gun-point. That's all that happened.

It is you, in your mind, in your limits, who put meaning and you create stories around that. You talk about the children, you talk about negativity, you talk about how you're not safe anymore and you make up stories to make yourself a victim. And you are not a victim. As long as you have God, you're not a victim.

In fact, I will be bold enough to say, that you are a winner. I have a motto and my motto is; *'I never lose. I either win, or I learn'*

It doesn't matter what happens in your life, you were designed for greatness. Things will happen, the question is: What meaning and stories are you putting behind that? For me, I'm choosing to focus every thought that I have on the blessings. I'm going to focus on having gratitude. I'm going to focus on love, compassion, and getting closer to my Creator. That's what I'm going to focus on.

What are you going to focus on? That's what you have to decide. In every single second, minute and hour, you get to choose what you want to focus on and that's the key to being a victim or to step into your greatness. It is what you focus on that is creating your reality, and what's creating your reality is what's creating your experiences. That's the circle you are going around in. Make a positive choice to focus on what you have that's working and what you're grateful for and that will open the doors for you to receive more things to be grateful for.

Notes:

CHAPTER 3

Where Are You Going

Let's look at your 5-year plan.

What does your 5-year plan look like?

Who is in it?

Where are you working?

What is your clothing style?

Who are the people that are around you?

Think more about what is around you - the sights, the smells.

How old are your children?

Are you traveling?

What do your vacation plans look like?

How many people are on your team or staff?

What does your body look like - are you healthy?

Think about everything that might be involved in what your life would look like in 5 years.

Switch gears for a minute and think about your 1-year plan.

Think about this exact day 12 months from now.

Where are you?

What does your life look like?

Who is in your life and what does your body look like now?

These exercises are all about your future self.

Think about everything - who you are connected to and even what kind of food you are eating.

Now, bring your thoughts to only 6 months from now and think about all of the same things.

What kinds of conversations are you having with yourself and others?

Where are you and who are you with?

What does your bank account look like?

Don't forget about your physical self - your body and your health.

What is important in your life now?

Where are your friends and family?

What are they doing?

The next topics will be incremental steps that are broken down by months and weeks. I will slowly take you through the steps. Are you ready? I know you will love it, so let's get started!

Give yourself permission to dream and dream big! Give yourself permission to be outrageous and audacious in your dreams. Think incredible thoughts and ask for anything your heart desires.

I have found that big dreams get big results! Dream about your money and investments. Dream about the person you're with - your spouse, your kids. Dream about where you live and the kind of car you drive. Dream about your spirituality and what you want to achieve. Dream big. Dream enormous!

In your journal, write about your dream life now!

Notes: ✑

Notes: ✍

CHAPTER 4

Motivation is for Suckers

One of the most common questions I get is, "Fatima, how do I stay motivated? I want to launch an online business; how do I stay motivated? I want to go on a health and wellness and I want to go to the gym; how do I stay motivated? I want to ignite my marriage; how do I stay motivated?"

This is a really important topic. I'm going to give you my take on why motivation sucks.

I'm going to tell you a personal story of mine on how motivation sucks and how I was able to create incredible success in my life without any motivation.

So, how do you actually create success? You bring your dreams to life. Whether it's health and wellness, money, an online businesses, or relationships; something is not working the way you want it to work and you're hoping that you're going to wake up one day and be totally motivated to make a change. You're going to wake up. But that day is not coming. Not until you make that change.

How would you feel if I said to you, okay, motivation is absolutely not necessary to get your goals and your dreams and to have incredible success in your life?

How did I go from a welfare mom of five, to being a #1 best-selling author, two times in one year, having amazing clients, money, and an incredible life of my dreams, and I was able to create all of that without motivation?

Motivation is absolutely not necessary to actually create success. Having a bigger house and more money just means you won the competition. But who's in the competition with? Because, you see, I don't consider you to be my competition, I don't. In fact, I don't consider anyone to be a competition. Now, don't get me wrong. I'm just showing up here today to be the absolute best version of myself. Nobody in my circle, nobody in my family, in my community is a competition to me, nobody. So, how was I able to do that?

Let's say you set a goal, and one of your goals is, "I want to be able to get in the best shape of my life. I want to go running and I want to go to the gym." And so, everyone tells you all these different things to do. Or how many people create New Year's resolutions? "I'm going to lose weight" and "I'm going to quit smoking" and I'm going to do this and I'm going to do that and they do this on January the 1st and within the first 3 weeks of setting your resolutions, people stop.

So does motivation suck? Absolutely motivation is actually a scam. It's a scam that somebody actually sold you telling you that you need to get motivated every day to make your dreams come true. You need to be motivated to work on your marriage. You need to be motivated to eat healthy. You need to be motivated to become a good parent. You need to be motivated to become a good provider. You need to be motivated to create success and happiness in your life. That's a scam that you've been sold.

Sorry, someone had to tell you.

What do you think about when you wake up every day? Do you have like a little doll and you wind up the doll and the doll's like, "Give me an S, give me a U, give me a C-C, E-S-S, success, success. You can do it, you can do it." Do you have one of those little things in your room?

You do not need motivation in your life to get the job done. You do not need motivation to achieve the mind, body and well-being that you're looking for. You do not need motivation to achieve a 7 figure lifestyle. You do not need motivation to be a great mom or a great dad. You don't need motivation to be a great spouse. You do not need motivation in any area of your life. You do not need motivation to be a good servant to your Creator.

Where do you need motivation in your life? Do you need motivation to cook food for your children and for your family because they're hungry? If you're a mom and you're home or you're a dad and your baby needs their diaper changed; do you need motivation to change that? Do you need motivation? Studying? Why do you need motivation in your life to study? Do you need someone to go, "come on, come on, I'm a cheerleader and you're going to have success and rah, rah, rah." Why do you need motivation to start a dream business? I don't need motivation to pray my prayers. I don't need motivation to be a good mom or a good coach or a good spouse. I don't need motivation to wake up every day and build my business.

The origin of doing anything to change your life comes from inside. So here's the thing, why does motivation suck? Because it's a scam. The media has convinced you that you need to be motivated to do something that's actually good and beneficial for you and your families.

If you pray your prayers, how will you benefit your family and you? If you finish your studies, how will you benefit your family and yourself? If you actually launch your online business, how will you benefit you and your family?

This is what you need to do; you must be a woman or a man of your word. If you say you want to join the gym then you do it. Not because of the motivation from outside because here's the thing, you can be married to a great person and then they divorce you and now your motivation died. You can have something on the outside of you, if you put your eggs in that basket and that basket leaves, you will be left with nothing.

You must build your inner resources inside of you. You must build your inner resources that you don't need motivation outside of you. Your motivation comes from your inner drive. Your motivation comes from your why. Why do you want to have a great body? Why do you want to lose weight? Why do you want to make 7 figures online? Why do you want to have a great marriage, right? Why do you want to go and make 7 figures? Why do you want to be a great mom or a great dad? Why do you want to be a great servant to God? Why? And so, inside of you, you have to understand your why. Then, your why becomes your word which becomes your honor, motivation is a scam that you've been sold on.

Do you think that when your baby wakes up and your baby's hungry do you need to say "Oh my God, I need Fatima to come and motivate me so I can cook food for my children. I need Fatima's resources to motivate me so I can go change my baby's diaper. I need Fatima to motivate me so I can build myself and incredible life and an amazing life and I can be the best spouse and I can be the best sister and a mother and I can be the best servant of God because I need Fatima to motivate me because if she doesn't motivate me, my life is over."

Motivation is a big load of useless garbage. You don't need motivation to breathe. You don't need motivation to drink some water. You don't need motivation to actually start having an online business that's incredibly successful. You don't need motivation.

You've got to start being so incredibly focused on what you want. Your motivation to be an amazing spouse is to have a beautiful, thriving, and incredible marriage. Your motivation to be an amazing parent is because you want children who are success, God-conscience leaders. Your motivation to actually create a successful, incredible, online business is because you want freedom; you want to have money to feed orphans and to feed hungry people.

You've got to keep your eye on the prize.

I once walked into a tea shop and this lady was giving samples of tea. Being a tea drinker, I love trying out all the different flavours. The lady behind the counter greeted me and said, "Hello, Ma'am, how are you today?"

And I looked at her and I said, "I'm awesome."

And she just looked at me with awe and said, "Oh my God, that's...it's so shocking that you would say that. Did something amazing happen in your life today that you're so awesome? Because whenever people come into the shop and I say 'Hey, how are you?' they say, 'Fine, thank you.'"

So, I said to her, "Of course something amazing happened; I woke up today and nobody put me 6 feet under." That could have happened to me this morning, but guess what? I'm alive. I have one more day to make a difference. I have one more day to put a smile on someone's face. I have one more day to sit and hug my children. I have one more day to have a conversation with incredible people like you."

I don't need anyone to motivate me. I wake up ready to start my day. I am waking up ready; igniting my life with fearless faith. When you wake up in the morning, you say, In The Name of God, and start your day. Start your day with magnificence. Start your day with courage. Start your day with strength and audacity and boldness and encouragement from the inside because motivation from the outside is a total scam.

People pay thousands of dollars for motivation. I believe that God has made us all accountants. That's all you are. Money is like energy. Money comes, money goes and the more you hold onto your money, the less will arrive. You've got to spend and share and give away for more money to come. It's just like water in a garden hose; if you step on it and you hold onto it, you're not going to get any more. You need to distribute your money to get more. The more you give, the more will come. And that's the same with love, the more you give, the more will come. If you hold on tight to your love, you can't get anymore. You've got to give it to get it. Give it to get it.

When I was on welfare, in 2009, I saved all the stubs from welfare, because it helped me to know where I was, where I was going. When I was stuck in that place without any money, it was $535.00 plus my son Tarik's disability check; that we survived on.

That's all we had.

When your children are hungry and you have left a multi-million dollar lifestyle and the entire community has abandoned you, you don't have motivation. You don't have any motivation because my heart and my head and everything was so sad all the time, and my children were asking me, "Was this the right move?"

I got onto the floor, found old recycled magazines, and I made myself a beautiful dream board where I took pictures from the recycle and garbage people had thrown away and I would cut out pieces form a magazine and I would stick it on this board.

And I had to really question myself like, "Did I leave this violent, abusive relationship for this?"

Was this the right move?

I created this dream board and that dream board was my why.

Why did I want this?

Why did I want to show my children what a healthy, happy and God-conscience parent looked like?

Why did I want to create my own money for my own freedom?

Why did I not want to rely on another human being because they all let me down?

Why did I want to show my children that I was so much more than just a woman who was abused?

Why did I want to show my children that I had more value? That's what motivated me.

I didn't need anything outside of me!

I held on to that dream. I held onto that why. Every day I woke up and I would re-create my why. I would ask myself, "Why do I want this?" and re-ignite the why and visualize what my life would look like when I success arrived. And that's what I did every day to build my inner resources, to build my self-esteem, to build my self-respect, to build my self-worth.

Even through my tears, I never let go of that dream. Even through my broken heart, I never let go of my dreams.

I refused to complain to God about all the things in my life that weren't working. I refused to tell God everything that was going on because you see; He already knew. What I did though, was I asked God for what I wanted. I asked God for the dream. I asked God to manifest my vision. I asked God for that, only which He could create, and no man would be able to give me and no woman would be able to give me, that's what I asked for.

I went to God and I begged with all of my conviction that I wanted my dream and vision to come true - if it was good for me, if it was good for my children, if it was good for my life and my hereafter; that He could open the way for me like he did for Moses in the sea.

I just knew that He would give me what I wanted because He loves us all so much. God will never deny you, your dreams. God will never deny you of what it is you want so bad, and your drive, and your vision, and your dedication, and your tenacity, he will never deny you. It is your job to create a relationship with God because he never left; you did.

With the passing of each day, my vision is changing. The people I'm helping are changing and inside of myself, my being, and my showing up is being reinvented. Every day and in every way we get better and better with God in your corner.

When you go through pain; that is the best time for you to reinvent yourself. When you go through pain, sit in your pain and ask Allah to use you. Ask Allah to use you for the greater good. You will be amazed at how Allah will use you to benefit the world, to benefit your bank account, to benefit your body, to benefit your relationships, and you get to show up clear.

Every time you go through pain, know that you are being cleansed of something and does it hurt? Yes, it hurts. Is it okay? Yes, it's okay. You need to go through that so you show us who you really are. You need to go through pain to reveal your essence. Ask Allah, "Use me. Use me to make the world a better place. Use me to bring a message forward to help the world. Use me Allah, to make the world a better place. Use me Allah, for the message of truth. Use me. Use me to help your servants." Remember, Muslims are not the only servants of God. Every single person walking on this planet is a servant of your creator, all of them. God has made all of them. God feeds every single person and you and I are just servants walking on this planet, making the world a better place. That's what you're doing; making the world better one prayer at a time!

Notes: ✑

_____

_____

_____

_____

_____

_____

_____

CHAPTER 5

Action Steps

Let's look at some action steps. Let's break down a year into 4 quarters. Take whatever month you're in right now and look ahead 3 months. Since there are 12 months in a year, you'll break down your year into three month intervals. Take each quarter and figure out how to go from where you are right now to where you want to be at the one year mark.

Suppose I want to lose 20 pounds in one year. How would I break this down into smaller, achievable intervals? Take the 12 months of the year and divide by 4 in order to get your quarter month marks. Take the 20 pounds I want to lose and divide it by 4, which means I need to lose 5 pounds every 4 months.

When you look at where you want to be in a year, it's easier to divide it up into smaller steps. Since I want to lose 20 pounds in 52 weeks (1 year), I can set a weekly goal that is much smaller than the 20 pounds. Now I can see that I only need to lose about half a pound each week. If you know what you want to achieve each week, you can make an action plan to get there. If you know where you're going, you'll get there!

20 (pounds) / 4 (quarters) = 5 pounds every four months =

Or

20 pounds / 52 weeks = 0.5 pounds a week

Now take a YEAR long goal you want to achieve and divide it into smaller increments that are achievable. And do this now.

Notes: ✍

CHAPTER 6

Blessings vs. Problems

Running around doing errands during the day and being able to be there for my children truly makes me appreciate being self-employed. I set my own hours and I take vacations whenever I want. I have been so blessed with the life I have been given.

Of course, there are times when life becomes overwhelming and challenging; but it is in those moments that you need a perspective change. The problem is that the majority of people concentrate on their problems. You concentrate on what's not working in your life and on the things that are causing us distress. But, what is the benefit of that?

You've really got to ask yourself; *"How does that benefit me? By focusing on my problems, where is it going to get me?"* When you really think about what you are blessed with in your life and take some time to count your blessings, I can almost guarantee you that your blessings will outweigh your problems every single time.

In our busy, day-to-day lives, there is an ongoing battle between blessings vs. problems. The bottom line is; what you focus on is what you get more of. And so, when you focus on your problems, you'll see more "problems" arise in every situation. Ask yourself this; what you focus on when you wake up in the morning? What takes up most of your energy? Is it a sense of amazement, happiness and the thought that *'yes, my life is working'*? Or is it the opposite of that where you tell yourself that nothing in life is working? Are you worried about paying the bills? Are you worried about a conversation that you don't want to have? Are you worried that you might be getting fired? Maybe you tell yourself that nothing is working. What are you focusing on?

If you take a deeper look into yourself, you will see that there are areas in your life where you can change. If you had a magic wand that could grant you anything, what would you want for yourself? Would you want to lose 100 pounds? Get married? Become an entrepreneur? Be rich and successful?

So, the question is; what are you doing about it? What's that *one step* that you must take to turn that possibility into a reality? There are countless times when you have told yourself that the dreams and goals you have must be achieved by tomorrow. You all want quick results. But more often than not, things in life take time and effort. The only thing you need to do by tomorrow is make a different choice.

When life hits you with all its might, take a few minutes to reflect. Ponder over your blessings. Try to think of 10 things that you are incredibly grateful for. They don't have to be big things. Perhaps you are grateful for your family, your delicious food, your cozy bed, or merely the ability to breathe.

My son Tariq is in a wheelchair. He cannot open the fridge, he cannot get a drink of water from the tap by himself, he cannot get into the shower, nor can he go to the bathroom by himself.

Imagine if you were given that test. A test where you are confined to a wheelchair for life; what would that be like for you?

Often, when it comes to blessings, you have the tendency to focus on the big things and overlook the small. You tell yourself *"I'm only going to be grateful if..."* but, that is not the only time to be grateful. There are many small things that you can be grateful for.

Many times, when I ask my clients, *"What are you grateful for?"* they actually have a hard time thinking about what they are grateful for. However, if I ask the question, *"What's not working in your life?*

What's troubling you? What's challenging you?" they can name 20 things off the top of their head. And so, what does that tell you? It tells you what you focus on!

The moment you acknowledge your blessings, is the moment your problems will start to seem insignificant. The more you focus on your blessings, the more you will see all your "problems" as blessings in disguise. It is easy to focus your energy on the negative instead of the positive. If you put your attention entirely on the negative, you will amplify the negativity because in every scenario, it will be the only thing you see.

Take your problems, your negativity and all the bad energy and put it into one box. Then, take all your blessings, positivity and good vibes and put them into a much bigger box. It is only then, that you'll see the true beauty of life even in the smallest of things and in the hardest of times.

Notes: ✍

_____

_____

_____

_____

_____

_____

_____

_____

Notes: ✍

CHAPTER 7
Why

Without judging yourself, did you really think about where you are in your life right now? Now let's look at the why. Why did you pick up this book? My guess is that you want something better for your life. Something better and bigger.

You want a healthy body, great relationships, money and success. You want to get closer to your creator and improve the relationships you already have. You want MORE out of your life and you've decided not to stay where you are! This book is about personal power and transforming your life. Now that you've figured out where you are in life, you can change it - if you want to!

It's time to make a decision. The time is right and the time is now. It's time to figure out *why*.

Get in the present and ask yourself the really hard questions. Why do you want to change your life? Why do you want to change your relationships? Why do you want that car or money?

When things in your life are amazing and everything seems to be going right, you don't need to tap into your WHY. But when you experience days when you just don't want to get out of bed and do anything, those are the days you will need this. Here's your opportunity to tap into your *what* and *why*. What do you really want? Do you want to leave a legacy and make a difference? Do you want to show your family that you are more than they think you are? It's time to prove it.

When you are writing your "why", tap into what you want to be known for when you die. What do you want people to say about you?

One of the things I want people to say about me is that I made a difference. I want people to say I believed in them even when they didn't believe in themselves. I want it to be on the right side of my good deeds scale. When I am judged in front of my Creator, I want my legacy to continue. I want to create a revolution of truth and service that continues after I've made my transition. I want my children to see me as more than just a woman that experienced violence. These are my reasons *why*.

On those days, where I couldn't get out of bed and was so tired that I didn't want to do anything. On those days when my business wasn't working. On those days when I had lost all my motivation and fear and doubt would creep into my thoughts. On those dark days, I would read my list of *why* I wanted to do this, and it kept me going. This your opportunity.

In your journal, write your *why*. Do it now!

Notes: ✍

CHAPTER 8

Thoughts

Take a minute to really think. How do your thoughts control what you do? Every day, people have ideas that provide a solution to someone's pain, close a gap, make something work better in their own life, or just to make the world a better place to live in. All of these ideas and inventions led to the creation of programs, facilities, campaigns and businesses that started with just a single thought.

Take another minute to think about your own life. What things do you think about? There are so many thoughts that are not beneficial and do not help you move in a positive direction. Yet, you are the one, thinking these things and ultimately controlling your future! Whether you like it or not, you are creating your life through your thoughts. You tend to "go with the flow" of life, not realizing how your unconscious thoughts control you.

When I look back at my own life, I realize that almost all of the decisions made before the age of fourty, were based on fear. Fear of loss; fear of someone not liking me; fear of not being accepted; and fear of someone getting angry with me.

I was raised to be a "good girl" and to be obedient. I had no idea what it was like to realize I had my own thoughts! Instead of ideas that came from a place of creation and possibility, they came from a defense mechanism and a fear of making others angry with me. Here is YOUR opportunity to look at your life and write down your thoughts. Thoughts about getting things done. Thoughts about what to say in a conversation, what to do in a confrontation, and how to handle others not agreeing with you. Write down all of the thoughts that you have about how to create the things you want in life.

Take a minute now and write down all those thoughts in your journal. Do that now!

So now what? What do you do with the thoughts that you've written down? You might be looking at them thinking "Oh my god, are these the thoughts that I have in my life?" Or, "Is this what I say to myself when no one else is listening?" You might even wonder if your thoughts are cruel or mean. You might even wonder if this is how you abuse yourself with your mind when you're alone. So what do you do about it?

You do nothing.

Taking notice of these thoughts and engaging in awareness and observation is enough in itself to cause a transformation.

One of the things my former husband used to say to me is "Fatima, just shut up and sit there and look pretty. I didn't marry you for your brains, I married you for your beauty. Nothing you have to say benefits anybody, so shut up!"

I believed every single word that he said as though it was the truth. I learned to be quiet. I learned to be an obedient wife. When I left that violent, abusive relationship, I had to reprogram my brain. I had to reprogram my thoughts.

In 2009, I found myself on my own with a need to reprogram my brain and all of my thoughts. One of the statements that I used was:

Every time I open my mouth, someone benefits. Every time I speak, I say something that is beneficial and helpful.

Now is an opportunity for you to carve out and write down statements that you want to become true for you. The key to this is making sure it is done from a place of gratitude. Every time you open your mouth, think about the fact that you are saying something beneficial and helpful. Your statements must come from thinking that it's already a done deal. They should not come from a place of thinking, I'm on my way to doing it, or I'm going to, or I'm willing to. You must realize that you're already doing it.

For example, if you want to lose weight, your statement might be: "thank you, I love my healthy, sexy body."

If you want to get out of debt, your statement might be: "thank you, I'm so grateful that I have more money than I can spend and I will share and spend my money and give it to charity."

Or if you want to own your own coaching business like, Million Stars Academy Certification Coaching Program, your statement might be: "thank you, I'm so grateful that I have this incredible coaching program, my clients are amazing, they spend money on their personal development, my clients are fun and do their homework, and I love my coaching business because I am making a difference for so many women in my community and online."

Finally, if you want to have a great relationship with your children and family, your statement might be: "thank you, I love the relationship I have with my husband, my children, and my friends, and our conversations are so open that we can talk about anything and everything, and I love every minute of interacting with them because I feel supported, loved and included."

Now, open up your journal and write down all the statements in your life that you want to be true. Make it real. Make it positive. Make it in the present tense. Do it now!

Notes: ✑

CHAPTER 9

Making a Decision

If you are still reading this book, you have reached the point where I know that you are committed to your greatness, freedom, and personal power. You could stop reading. You could stop at this point in the book and create an incredible life that is extraordinary, abundant and unleashed. This is the bridge where you get to make a decision as to whether or not you are going to continue reading the rest of this book. Now is when I get to help you be the change the world is so desperately needing!

Now is when I get to help you create a coaching business with people who are paying billions, not millions, of dollars for! Now is when I get to help you cross the bridge and make a decision to create an incredible online and offline coaching business! Now is the time for you to take a stand and be a Million Stars coach!

I will show you step-by-step how to do this, but first it's time for you to make a decision. Are you saying yes? Are you saying yes so loudly that the world and universe start conspiring to send everything your way?

Isn't it amazing and absolutely incredible when you give yourself permission to say yes to becoming a coach?

Say it loud - I am now choosing to have an outstanding, extraordinary and wildly successful coaching business!

You are not going to get stuck on all the strategies and action steps that will come later, because right now you are simply making a solid decision to say yes to your future.

Are you saying yes or no?

What is your choice going to be?

In your journal, write down exactly what you are choosing.

I am choosing to be a Certified Million Stars Coach. Write your decision in big, black, bold letters. Use whatever colored pens you can find and write it out in as many places as you can. I am choosing to say yes to my future!

I am choosing to be a million stars coach.

I am choosing to make a difference.

I am choosing to be part of this revolution of truth and freedom to help women globally.

I am choosing to make more money than I've ever had in my life.

I am choosing to be extraordinary.

I am choosing to show my family who I really am.

I am choosing to get paid well and to have the best of the best of this world and the best of the best of the after-world.

You've made that decision and I'm so proud of you.

I acknowledge you for your greatness. I acknowledge you for your bravery. I acknowledge you for your courage. It takes courage to be different. It takes courage to be abundant. It takes courage to be brilliant and make a difference in the world. I acknowledge you and I want you to really feel my acknowledgment in your heart.

Really get how proud I am of the steps that you are taking to create an extraordinary life for you and the people around you. Wow!

Next steps it is time to visualize.

I mean really visualize a future that is complete amazing. A future where you have that amazing coaching business. You can see your coachees. You see your bank account. You see the numbers in your bank account getting bigger. You see yourself getting paid. You see happy clients getting wonderful results. You see the testimonials they send you by email. You hear your clients telling you what a difference you made in their lives.

Close your eyes and visualize that ideal life with the business of your dreams

Do this now!

Notes:

Notes: ✍

CHAPTER 10

Surviving the Situation

There are moments in life when it feels like everything around you is falling apart. You feel like there is nothing you can do to fix this situation. You feel pain, you feel hurt, and you feel broken. There are so many things happening in this world and often you get this thought that says, "I've never experienced something so bad in my whole life and just I don't know what to do." So, the question is; how do you survive a situation?

Every single individual is going through something today. There are people all over the world that are going through some kind of pain today. Whether you're going through a divorce, or you just got diagnosed with an illness, or you got fired from your job; there is always something going on in your life. It is important to take time and reflect over what is happening in your life that is making you feel as though you cannot survive the pain and make it through to the other side.

All around the world, there are people going through pain. Someone just found out that they got fired. Someone just found out that their Visa got revoked. Someone just found out that they have an incurable illness. Someone just found out that they're getting divorced. Someone just got rejected. Someone just got hurt. Someone just lost a person close to them. Someone lost their child. Someone lost their marriage. Someone lost their business. Someone lost their freedom. Regardless of what you are going through, you are experiencing an incredible amount emotional pain. There are things happening within you right now that you feel you have no control over and you're asking yourself, *"How do I manage this situation? How do I get over it because this emotional pain is hurting so much?"* You can't see the pain; it's not like a cut that you can apply a cream and wrap it with a bandage. This pain is in your heart. This pain is your body. This pain is in your very thoughts.

What I found in my life is, the moment I feel depressed or have a sense of hopelessness and helplessness, I go do something awesome for someone else. There are people in your neighborhood that you can help. There are family members that need your help. I take myself out of my own pain and I ask, *"Who can I help right now?"* because when someone else benefits, that gives me joy. That joy helps me to take the focus off myself completely. When I'm drowning in a world of hopelessness and helplessness, I catch myself playing victim. I start asking myself, *"Why me?"* and *"Why did this happen to me?"* I immediately dive into all the 'should have's' and 'could have's'. When I'm in that dark place of helplessness and hopelessness, all the attention is on me; I become blind to everything else, I just see me and my terrible situation. When I'm feeling completely powerless, I go do something amazing for someone else; even if it's something as small as smiling at someone.

Now, here's the thing that I have learned about surviving situations. No matter how difficult a situation may seem, if you look back six months or a year there was a situation in your life that, at that time, you thought you wouldn't be able to overcome; but you did! Just the same way, you will get through this situation and come out on the other side a stronger individual.

I've been in numerous situations where I thought, *"I am so broken right now. I have so much pain right now; I don't know how I'm ever going to survive."* In 2008, I left my marriage with 5 kids; a special needs child, my youngest was 4, my oldest was in University. I took them and I went into hiding. I had no money and that was a time in which I thought I would never be able to survive. I was engulfed in fear. But,

I knew and I believed that there was a Power bigger than me that would watch over me, guide me and provide for me. When I was full of despair, He saved me. When every single human let me down, He replaced them with people that could stand for me. In the same way, you will survive this situation. You will survive and you will thrive but only if you trust and surrender. As long as you are holding on to your pain, you will *never* enjoy the fruits that life brings your way.

Have you ever been or seen children playing in a park on the monkey bars? You can only get to the next bar if you let go of the first one. You will never be able to move on with your life if you don't let go of what you have right now. You will never move forward because you're holding on so tight to what you think is good for you, even though it may not be. How will you know until you trust the One who knows the unseen? It is He that has the knowledge of the past, the present, the future. He has the knowledge of the unseen and you and I, you don't even know what's happening behind your back.

You don't know what's happening even when you see it because even when you see things, you see things through your filters. You can only see things from your experiences. You can only see things from your paradigm.

From the glasses you are wearing is the only thing you get to see.

You don't know my perception. I don't know your perception. You don't know the third person's perception. You don't know how I see life. I don't know how you see life.

Don't go to your problems and tell them, "*I'm going to bring my big brother, I'm going to bring my husband, I'm going to bring my father*", go to all your problems, say, "*I'm going to bring Him.*" That's the moment when you stand tall with confidence, self-worth and self-respect. That's the day you become a winner. You let go of everything that you thought that you knew and you step into the world of your Creator.

Placing your faith in His hands doesn't mean everything will be rainbows and butterflies. The moment you decide that you are on His side, He will test you. He will test you to see if it's just lip service or whether you truly place your trust in Him. He will test you to see if you actually mean what you say. The rewards of these tests are absolutely incredible.

You will enjoy abundance from places that you never imagined. You will enjoy the fruits of your Creator in ways and possibilities that your two-dimensional life cannot imagine.

You will survive the situation you are in, *when* you change your attitude. You change who you are being. You can never solve the problem from the same attitude and energy as when you created the problem. You must create something new. The only way you do that is by having a coach or a mentor to give you a different way of being otherwise the problem keeps coming back wearing different shoes. Until such a time where you fix your way of being, you fix your patterns and belief system, you will keep getting the same results.

You can't expect to get a new flavor if you're using the same recipe. You need to tweak the recipe by adding a special ingredient that will make your taste buds burst with flavor. In the recipe of your life, you need to add a coach or mentor who can guide you and say, *"You might want to change this. You might want to add this. You might want to not add that. You might want to take a little bit of time doing this or that."* That's when you'll start discovering the all the beautiful flavours that life has to offer.

Your life has been working from a point of survival. Isn't it time to switch the gear from surviving to glorious and abundant? Isn't it time for you to be the author of your own life instead of just surviving because circumstances were thrown at you? Isn't it time for you to be fed-up of the way things have been? Look at the results of your life; that's how you know what kind of life you are leading. Look at your bank account. Look at your friends. Look at your attitude. Look at your body. Look at your career. Look at your finances.

If you are not living a life that you are authoring every single day, you're wasting your life away.

If you are not the pilot flying the plane of your life, you are barely in survival mode.

So, what exactly is 'survival mode'? Plain and simple, survival mode is *reaction*. There's never been a game, in any sports, that has been won in a defense mode. Never. The game is never won on the defense. The game is always won on the offense. You've got to score to win. You can't just block the shots; you've got to shoot some hoops in order to win. The game is always won on the offense and it's time for you to actually step into that. Be the one in the driver's seat. Buckle up, put the car in drive and steer your life in the direction that *you* want it to go in!

Notes: ✍

_____

_____

_____

_____

_____

_____

_____

_____

_____

Notes: ✎

CHAPTER 11

The World Needs You

Why have you decided to have a home-based coaching business?

Let's talk about that woman who needs a coach, and why she needs you right now. You may have noticed that there are a lot of families falling apart. Stress levels are high. People have a lot of money. Relationships are breaking down. The divorce rate is at an extreme high. The political climate is terrible.

Right now, as you are reading this, the world needs coaches. The world needs life coaches, business coaches, strategic coaches, executive coaches, health and wellness coaches, fitness coaches, relationship coaches and many more specialized coaches.

More than a billion dollars is spent on coaching alone. People understand there is a need to find someone to speak to, who is in your corner. And that person is not a doctor, but someone who is a coach.

Someone who has been trained to ask specific questions. To be an accountability partner. To listen to then, so they are heard. People are demanding this.

And you are in the best time of this planet to be a coach. You can do this full-time or part-time. You can do this from home or from an office. The power of online marketing from the comfort of your home while you're doing laundry, while you're raising your children, while you're at home busy with your family, or while you work at another job.

You can start this business and make six figures within your first year. You can create an amazing successful business while you make a difference and help other people.

There is no better model of business I have found for you to make a difference, leave a legacy, and transform lives. You get to impact and influence the world while you reach millions of people.

I have five children and I have a special needs son, Tarik. Tarik was diagnosed with cerebral palsy spastic quadriplegic, and he is in a wheelchair. There was no way possible for me to go work outside the home, and pay somebody to look after my son. I was able to create my business in such a way that I could stay home with him, look after him and create a wonderful business where I get to change lives and make money. This business has positioned me as an expert and as an influencer in my field. And you can do this too.

And so you might be wondering or asking yourself,

- What can I coach on?
- What's my expertise?
- I don't have experience
- I didn't go to school
- I don't have a certification
- Or anything else?

This is a good time for you to open your journal and write down all the questions that you are thinking about. Write down all the doubts, fears, worry and limitations. Go ahead and do that now.

Here's what will happen next…

A coach is someone who is kind, loving, empathetic and a person who can ask the right kind of questions so transformation is present.

I'm going to teach you:

- Exactly what kind of questions to ask a potential client.
- How do ask incredible powerful questions.
- How to create possibility.
- How to give your client awareness.
- How to make your client conscious of where she is, and what's happening in her whole world.
- How to be a mirror so you get to listen to her and have her feel heard.
- And all other types of questions.

That is your job as a coach.

You job as a coach is to listen. I mean really listen. And after listening, your job is to ask powerful questions.

Can you be that loving space and container where she can feel safe to express herself freely? Can you give her the opportunity to feel heard?

I know you can. I am absolutely certain and confident that you have already done that. You have been that girl who everybody comes to. They speak to you about their problems. You are the girl that everybody comes and dumps all their problems on. Right?! You are the girl that people trust. You have been the girl that people have come to, and you have gone out of your way to help others.

You have always been that girl.

Look at your life. Look at all the times that people have come and confided in you because they trusted you. Look at the times in your life when you helped people. You've already done that! Look back at your life and remember all the times that you helped by listening and comforting another person.

The only difference is you didn't know how to market yourself. You didn't how to get paid for it. You didn't know this was a business model. You didn't know that you could actually facilitate transformation. And you probably didn't know the exact powerful questions to ask.

Well, I've got some amazing news once again. You're in the right place, and this is the right time for you.

Let's get started teaching you how to formulate a business that is a viable. A business that is going to give you more money than you can spend. A business where you get to create transformation for others. A business when you leave a legacy. A business that you can do part-time or full-time. A business that you can do, without needing to spend 10 years in university.

Welcome to your new life!

Notes: ✎

CHAPTER 12

Mirroring

One of the most powerful techniques that you can use in your coaching business is called "mirroring"

Mirroring is also called re-flection, and is also called repeating. Repeating what someone says is also called "having the other person feel gotten" or "being heard".

Why is mirroring and reflection so important? Problems happen in relationships when people feel they have not been heard. Business relationships, intimate relationships, family, children, parents etc. It happens in all relationships. When people feel that they have not been heard, they feel dismissed. And the most powerful way to bypass that is to have people be heard.

I'll give you an example in a real-life situation. My son came home and said, "Mommy, I've got all of these things to do. I've got a project to do. My friends want to go out. I need my haircut. My glasses are broken. And, I'm really asking for some help here!"

The old me would have said, "okay okay, let's go get it done. Let's make the appointment…!" and I would have swept in and fixed everything.

The new me said, "What I'm hearing you say is that you got an assignment, you've got this project, your friends want to go out, your glasses need fixing, and you need to go get a haircut! Did I hear you correctly?"

He answered, "Yeah yeah. You did"

Then I said, "Okay great. How can I help you? Can I support you in any way?"

He answered, "No. I'm fine. I just want you to know what's happening. And if you don't see me, then I'm good, and I'll be gone for the day."

In the new situation I'm asking questions rather than providing a solution like I used to do. This gives me and my son, the space and freedom to see what he wants. I have the privilege of getting into his world, and he feels heard and supported.

Mirroring helps you to be in the world of your clients. People want to be heard so when you reflect, and use the mirroring technique with compassion and love, the other person feels heard. And when they feel heard, they feel safe.

It's truly amazing how people come up with their own solutions when we mirror them, and ask questions.

Most of the time when you provide a solution from your perspective, it's coming from your world, and you think that's best for your clients. Studies have now shown, that the person is more likely to create change and transformation in their life, if the solution comes from within them. And this is excellent news for coaches, because you are not playing the role of a mentor, a psychologist, or a consultant who provides solutions. Coaches don't tell people what to do. Coaches simply facilitate change through a series of powerful questions.

Coaches move people from where they are in their stuck-ness, to where they want to go to achieve their goals and dreams.

Coaches help their clients to navigate to other side of the bridge, metaphorically speaking.

Notes: ✍

Notes: ✍

CHAPTER 13

Niche

How to start a coaching business from home. Step one: Decide what type of coach you want to be. What kind of people do you want to help? Is it a life coach? Are you a business coach? Or any other kind of coach like

- Weight-loss coach,
- Fitness coach,
- Health coach,
- Parenting coach,
- Relationship coach,
- Wealth coach,
- Productivity coach,
- Organizational coach,
- Technical coach,
- Sales coach,
- Career coach.
- And so many more other types of coaches.

There is a plethora of specialized coaches you can choose from.

I love being a specialist coach. I spend a one year specializing as a "Divorced-Muslim-Women Coach". Being a specialized coach, took my business to six figures in one year. During that one year, I wrote books, wrote articles, made videos, and spoke only on that niche.

Being a specialist positioned me to become an authority and an expert in that field. I quickly became the speaker and coach for anyone looking for that specialty. Instead of being a jack-of-all-trades, and getting lost in the chaos of all other coaches, I stood out.

Choose a niche where you can be seen as an expert. Establishing your niche will help you to easily identify your avatar.

At this point, you may be feeling a bit worried that if you specialize, you will not make money.

Please take out your journal and write down all your fears about creating a narrow, tiny, micro-specialization.

Do this now.

Notes: ✍

_____

_____

_____

_____

_____

_____

_____

_____

Great work.

Now it's time for you to write down what your niche is. How do you discover your niche? Here are some ideas:

- What lights you up?
- What do you talk about non-stop?
- What have you studied?
- What are your life experiences?
- What do others come and speak to you about?
- What are you always giving advice on?
- Who are you for other people?
- What books do you like to read?
- What courses have you taken?
- Where have you travelled?
- What pain have you experienced?
- What adversities did you overcome?

Take out your journal and answer the above questions.

Do that now.

Notes: ✍

_____

_____

_____

_____

_____

_____

Look at all your answers. What have you written? What is the niche that you are choosing? Write that down now.

Notes: ✍

Once you've established your niche; don't worry if you feel like this is confining.

Nobody wants a coach that is a 'generalist'. The general coach gets paid 'general money', and the specialist gets paid, the top dollar.

Now time to find your ideal client. Who is she? You must know her, better than she knows herself. Get into her world, her thoughts and her fears.

Answer the following questions:

- How old is she?
- Is she married?
- Is she single?
- Is she a homeowner or does she rent?
- Where does she live? In the city? In the suburbs?
- Where does she shop?
- Is she a yoga fanatic?
- Does she exercise?
- What magazines does she read?
- Does she work?
- Is she a stay-at-home mom?

- Does she home-school?
- What shows does she watch?
- Are her kids at university?
- What are her dreams?
- What does she worry about?
- Is she looking after aging parents?
- Does she have investments?

Be as specific as you can.

Notes: ✍

_____

_____

_____

_____

_____

_____

_____

_____

_____

This is critical. You must know her, to be her coach.

This information will be used to:

- Write copy
- Write email
- Create Facebook statuses
- Write tweets
- Make videos
- Create programs
- Write a book
- Speak on stage
- Create a pitch.

Why is this important?

When your ideal client is watching your videos or reading your Facebook status; one of three things must be happening in her mind.

- Number one, she says, "wow that's exactly what I need in my life".
- Number two, she says, "nope that's not for me",
- or number three she says, "I know exactly who needs this you"

You don't want tire kickers and people 'thinking about your services'. You don't want people who are wishy-washy and sitting on the fence.

This is a REAL business and the key ingredient for your success is to understand the fears of your ideal client, also known as your avatar.

- What does she worry about?
- What is the first thing on her mind?
- Is she worrying about her body?
- Is she worried about money?

- Is she worried about health and losing weight?
- Is she worried about immigrating to another country?
- Is she worried about keeping her children be safe?
- Is she worried about education?
- Is she worried about her neighborhood?

Whatever that specific worry is, you must provide a solution for her pain and worry.

In your journal, write down all her worries and fears.

Do that now.

Notes: 🖎

Notes: ✍

CHAPTER 14

Certification

Being a certified coach is not a requirement, but it can help you to become a fantastic coach.

Coaching certification will provide you with helpful coaching and marketing tools to get known.

Million Stars Academy trains women to become A Certified Million Stars Coach, where you will be immersed in a 12-month online training program. Every month you will receive a new module with teachings and assignments with milestones and deadlines. The modules teach you everything you need to know about mastery, marketing, modules, media, mindset and money.

It also includes modules on, how do you grow a team and how do you write a book to position yourself as a number one best-selling author. How to get the speaking gigs and clients. How to price your own teaching modules. What is group coaching? What is a mastermind? What is a VIP day? And how to set your prices for those.

When you arrive at The Million Stars Academy website, the first thing you will see is a giant global map with stars flickering on it. These stars will show you where all the certified Million Stars Coaches are in the world.

There will also be "member-only" for the coaches to access a back-office. In the back-office, you can access all the teaching modules and up-to-date training of the best practices that is happening in the coaching industry. Your certification will give you credibility under the Million Stars banner

Million Stars Academy will do all the advertising to feature our certified coaches, so you never have to worry about getting clients.

Users will easily find a coach in their neighborhood by scanning the global map and finding a coach close to them or finding a global coach that specializes in the niche they desire.

In your journal, write what that experience will be like to be supported as a coach, in The Million Stars Academy.

Do that now

Notes: ✐

_____

_____

_____

_____

_____

_____

_____

_____

_____

_____

CHAPTER 15

A Name

Claiming your business name is exciting and fun.

You could be thinking that getting a name is a daunting task because all the names are taken. Anything I want in my coaching business is already taken, and that is farthest from the truth.

Let's look at who you are. How unique you are. How special you. Who you are as a person and how your experiences have shaped you. How the Creator made you. Your size, your shape, your height, your language, where you come from, your experiences, your siblings, what schools you went to, all make you special and unique.

You are unique in the way you speak, your vocabulary, the sound of your voice, your voice inflection, the volume of your voice, the pitch of your voice, and how you deliver your message.

Everything is unique and special about you. All your experiences have brought you here. How you solve a problem, and how you coach and facilitate the change in a client also makes you unique.

Choosing a name for your business could be your own name or consider using a word that describes the results someone would get from working with you.

Some examples are:

- Fatima Omar Coaching
- Lifestyle Coaching
- High Performance Coaching

- Get Fit & Fabulous Coaching
- Abundance Coaching

In your journal, write down at least 10 ideas for your business name.

Do that now.

Notes: ✍

_____

_____

_____

_____

_____

_____

_____

_____

_____

_____

_____

CHAPTER 16

Choosing Your Business Structure

When it comes to choosing the structure of the business, it's always a good idea to speak to your accountant and lawyer in your area.

Do your research. The answers are different in different countries.

You have some choices:

- Sole proprietorship
- Corporation
- LLC in the USA
- A small business

When I first started my business, I began without creating anything special. I started coaching and would use Paypal to bill my clients. It was simple and easy.

Take one day at a time.

Different structures offer legal protection and come with different tax obligations. Make sure that whatever you using right away is you'll be able to pay taxes, and serve your clients in the best way possible.

Study how laws work in your country regarding which business structure is best for you.

Notes: ✍

CHAPTER 17

Home Vs Office

You've got your name. You've got your structure. How do you start providing service to clients?

Some people will want everything "perfect", and look for an office. Others will set up a space in their home.

You might decide to rent a space, get an 800 toll-free number and get a secretary. Your clients can find you at your office. And you're ready for business.

You might decide to work from home. You transform one of your bedrooms into an office space. Or maybe taking half a room or an area in one room, install a curtain to create space to work.

Get a small desk and set up a computer. You will need a printer and a good phone to make calls.

You also need a great internet connection.

You don't want your space to be messy, dirty or filled with laundry.

You want to create a space that you like. A space where you can be *the coach*.

And when you're done, you get to go and be mom, cook, and all the other roles you have in your life.

It's good idea to go online and have a look at some "home-office" ideas.

In your journal, write down your ideas for your office.

Do that now.

Notes: 🖎

_____

_____

_____

_____

_____

_____

_____

_____

_____

_____

_____

_____

_____

_____

_____

CHAPTER 18
Equipment

Your office is now set up. Congrats!

What equipment and online software do you need?

Let's talk about the different ways of delivering coaching.

- One-on-one coaching
- Live Group Coaching
- Taped Modules

For one-on-one coaching and group coaching, you need:

- a microphone
- Skype to see your people
- Zoom for recording video
- Instant Tele seminar for recording sessions and creating webinars

For Facebook Live videos, you need:

- An iPhone or an any kind of smartphone
- A Facebook account
- Great Connection

For Email marketing you need:

- An effective auto responder such as mailchimp, Infusionsoft, A Weberor any other CRM.
- Do NOT use your gmail account because that is called SPAM. And no-one likes spam.

For clients to book a session with you using an online calendar, you need:

- Calendy or Acquity or any one online calendar that allows you to set up your office hours, and helps you to receive payments.

A side-note with calendars. Make sure you add all your family events on the calendar first.

In your journal, write down all the action steps you will take this week from this chapter.

Do that now.

Notes: ✍

_____

_____

_____

_____

_____

_____

CHAPTER 19

Building The Website

Building the website is always so much fun and excitement! A good way to plan out your site is to actually look at how other people have done their websites. Look for coaches and others in the same field. Do a Google search and see who else is out there in your market. Whether you're a health and wellness coach, a business coach, an executive coach, a marriage coach, a diet coach, or whatever kind of coach are, just go out there and look for other people that are doing similar things. As you look at other people's websites, do not, I repeat, DO NOT copy anybody else's website! Chances are they have insurance and liability and you might get sued!

So what are you looking for in other people's websites? Inspiration! The first thing you will want to take note of are the colors. You might like certain colors that you feel attracted to and that make you feel nice. Maybe it's pinks and greens or maybe it's blues and yellows, everybody has an eye for what is beautiful to them, and if you can wear it with confidence, then your clients will no doubt pick up on that.

The next thing to look at is what kind of tabs for navigating the sections of your website.

Good tabs to have as a rule of thumb are things like "about me" where people can find a little bit about your background and what kind of solutions you provide.

Another good tab to have is something like "work with me" where clients can find information about how to work with you or how to book appointments through your online calendar. You might want to offer the first few months for free with 15 minute or 30 minute sessions, for example. The idea is to really get people to try you out, so it's good to give out complementary discovery calls that will draw people in.

Another very common tab for your website could be "testimonials", where clients can read statements from people that you have worked with, and beautiful pictures of satisfied clients!

The last tab is typically a "contact me" tab where people can contact you about who they are, what kinds of problems they are having, and what kinds of things are going on in their lives.

Let's talk about an 'lead-magnet", and how to build your list. You build your list by asking people for their email addresses. Most people won't just give away their email addresses for free.

So, how did I build my list? I gave them either a CD, a free report or a free book. After all, free stuff draws people in. And this is the law of reciprocity; you give a free report and they give you an email address.

In this chapter you will decide whether you want to create a report or CD. This must be done before you get to the next chapter. Every free report that you create or the free CD that you create must provide ample information on the coaching that you provide.

Here are some ideas of a lead magnet:

- If you're a confidence coach, it could be about how to be confident and raise your self-esteem.
- If you're a wellness coach, it could be something like, "How to include juicing in your diet to become healthier".

- If are a marriage coach, maybe "10 steps to create an amazing marriage in the next 60 days".

When people click on what you're offering, you ask for their email addresses, which allows them to receive the free offer.

Ask your webmaster to set that up.

When a visitor first arrives to your website, the very first thing they see is your free offer to draw them in. It will be shouting at them to join the community. Strategies like this will allow you to build a list of email contacts which consistently grows through free offers, calendar appointments, and your social media presence.

In your journal, write down the tabs you want for your website and the titles of the free offers you want to use to draw in potential clients. What value can you give these people to show them you are the expert and the authority that they need in their life?

Do this now.

Notes: 🖎

_____

_____

_____

_____

_____

_____

_____

Notes: ✍

CHAPTER 20

Marketing, Marketing, Marketing

There's a really great question that people often ask: "do you think that you could make a better hamburger than McDonalds?" Almost every single person has always said "Yes! Of course! They make junk!" So why is it that McDonald's has served over a billion people? Young children recognize those golden arches from an early age; even before they can read. It's all about marketing. You have to market! Market everywhere using social media, and online and offline strategies to get the attention of todays' consumer. We live in a fast-moving information-based economy; and your job is to *stand out.*

When I first started out, the three platforms that I chose were YouTube, Twitter and Facebook. I spent time learning about these platforms, and making sure to learn about each of them.

If you are a career coach, maybe LinkedIn could be one of the three that you choose; maybe Facebook isn't your ideal location.

If you are a beauty coach, or a cosmetic coach, you might teach makeup tutorials. In this case, Instagram could be a good choice.

If you are a creative coach who shows people how to draw or how to start their own business, Pinterest could be a good way to go.

Ask yourself, "Where do I need to focus my attention and how can I be consistent with my marketing?"

Whatever you choose, consistency is the key. Your reach must be great. You must be seen everywhere, all the time. If you choose Facebook, for example, you should be posting updates twice a day. You should make sure you have posts which are funny, posts that are personal, and, of course, posts that are relative to the work you are doing.

Also, follow others who are also coaching in your niche. There are no competitors out there if they are all collaborators. Follow these people and watch what they are doing not to copy them, but to be inspired by what they are doing to get an idea of how you can market yourself. You're out there producing and contributing free content to help people know that you are the one. That way, when people are looking for that particular niche, you will be the first name that comes up.

Another way to market is to write a book. My book, "How To Be a Muslim Woman Divorced and Totally Confident hit number one on Amazon. That same year I wrote: "From Ex to Extraordinary: How to Use Your Divorce as a Springboard for Success". Writing two bestsellers in the same year, solidified my position as an authority and an expert in that niche. Everyone who was looking for a divorce coach looked to me for guidance because I was seen as the authority in that niche.

Your reports, your books, your Facebook live, your Pinterest, your Instagram posts, your Tweets, your LinkedIn profiles must all match the conversation you are having in regards to your niche. They must be connected and use the same profile picture.

This is about consistency and branding.

When people see you on different platforms, they will see your face and your name. They will know who you are, and you get to create a brand and an identity that is completely congruent across all platforms.

In your tweets, in your Facebook, in your Pinterest, in your Instagram, on your LinkedIn, you are the same person everywhere. The more people see you, the more they see the content that you're providing, the more they see your face everywhere, the more they see you, the more you are known.

That is the way marketing is done and none of this comes at any monetary cost to you. Social platforms don't cost money!

Open your journal now and write all the different places online that you see your message being heard.

Do that now.

As you are doing this, think about your avatar; your ideal client.

Ask yourself "Where does she hang out?" is she on Instagram. That's where you need to be. Does she use LinkedIn? Then that's where you need to be. Does she use Facebook? Then, that's where you need to be.

You might eventually be on six different social media platforms, and that's okay. Start with three. What are your three top choices? Decide now, which are your top three choices for online social media platforms, and write down your ideas that are being inspired in you right now.

Start dreaming a little. If you could write a book, what should the title of your book be? What about the title of your CD? I'll give you a hint: the title of your Facebook post, the title of your free report you're offering, they're all going to be very similar. They're all solutions based on the problem that you're solving for your client.

So, if you're a sexual trauma coach then it would be how to heal after sexual trauma.

If you're a divorce coach, it could be how to find confidence.

If you're a marriage coach, maybe six ways to ignite the spark in your marriage again.

If you're a career coach, maybe three things people do to sabotage themselves and how to stay away from them.

If you're a health and wellness coach, perhaps how to drink more water.

Go ahead now and write down the three platforms you are choosing now.

Notes: 🖎

_____

_____

_____

_____

_____

_____

_____

_____

_____

_____

CHAPTER 21

Unique Selling Proposition

What is your unique selling point? In other words, what is your thirty-second elevator-pitch? How do you answer when people ask what you do? What I find, usually, is that people can be very general.

Most coaches will say something like "I can help you create an extraordinary life!" or "I can help your dreams come true!", or "I can help you get whatever it is that you want!" These responses are very generic, and it is simply crazy to think that somebody would buy it. These pitches do not have any imagination!

People want you to tell them exactly what you do.

With branding, you want to get every potential client to say one of three things.

1. "Yes, I want it! This is for me!"
2. "Nope, no thanks, not for me."
3. "I definitely know somebody that could use the service".

When your client sees your branding in an article or in a video, or at a networking function, she will know who you are.

My market was divorced Muslim women. I would hear people ask me "What do you do?" I would say that "I help divorced Muslim women release their pain, shame and guilt so that they can re-create their life, rediscover who they are, and make more money than their male relatives".

Your pitch must touch the pain you are helping them to release and also the hope and dreams they are looking for.

When people ask me "What is Million Stars?" I say, "Million Stars Academy is a coaching, certification program, where help one million women globally, regardless of race, religion, ethnicity or cultural background to create a viable coaching business so she can have the money and choices she deserves".

Now it's your turn to create a unique selling point. A short, succinct excellent thirty-second elevator pitch.

How do you help them solve that problem? Your unique selling point, your thirty-second elevator pitch, will specifically identify your audience, as well as the goals and the challenges of what you're solving in your own words.

This is how you position yourself. This is how you say "Hey! This is what I do! Come and check it out! I am the authority! I am the expert!"

In your journal, brainstorm your thirty-second elevator pitch. Here is the template:

I help _____ (audience), to release/let go/give up _____ (the pain, the worry), and help them get _____ (the goal, the dream).

It should clearly identify your audience, the problems that you are solving, and how you will be solving those problems.

Go ahead and write your 30-second elevator pitch now.

Notes: ✍

Notes: ✍

CHAPTER 22

Social Proof

Let's talk about building social proof. What does that mean? Building social proof?

Social proof is when third-parties endorse you. Social proof is testimonials. Clients sending you videos, and written comments saying how great you are.

You might be saying "Come on! I don't have any clients! I'm just building my business! How am I supposed to create social proof and get testimonials?"

Answer: Complementary Discovery Calls.

Create a contest. Create a game. You can give 30 minute sessions or complementary discovery calls for those wanting to apply. Put a limit on it. Say there's only 20 sessions available, where people can get free sessions in exchange for short testimonial videos. Get them to include things like how it felt working with you, how great you are, what you did for them, how you solved their problem.

Go after your ideal clients. They've got the money to pay you. They have the problem, they want your help.

Set up an appointment! Tell them that you're starting out and you want to be able to give them a coaching call for free in exchange for a testimonial.

Be upfront with them and let them know exactly what's going on. Have a real call, I mean a real call, with the real issue. Then you're free to create a solution for them! This is how you become an amazing and incredible coach.

This is an opportunity for you to practice and help people in real life situations!

You can record the calls, you can send the recordings to your clients, building trust and confidence. Your audience will see you as an expert, because that's who you are.

You can use your testimonials, and parts of the recorded calls with the permission of your client. Potential clients will listen to the recordings and say "Oh my God, this is the most amazing thing ever!"

On the call with your new client, invite them to join your three-month starter package. It would be perfect for them!

Multiple aspects are already happening, here on this complimentary free 30 minute call.

- First, you're getting a testimonial video or written testimonial.
- Second, you can record the call and get permission from the client that you could use.
- Third, at the end of the call, you can offer them the three-month starter package to get them started in a paid program with you as their coach.

When you receive those testimonials, you can put them on your testimonial page for social proof! How cool is that? I know, it's just amazing!

In your journal, write down what your new three-month coaching package looks like. The results that clients get after working with you for three months, the value, and what you will charge.

Do that now.

Notes: ✍

Notes:

CHAPTER 23

The Discovery Call

One day before the call, send your client an email to confirm the appointment.

2 hours before the call, read the online questionnaire they filled out to get familiar with her pain and her dreams.

Always call into the line 5 minutes before, so you are early.

Get related for the first 5 minutes.

Then get right into the questions.

- What's the biggest issue in your life right now?
- What's worrying you the most you wake up in the morning?
- What is her dream?
- Why does she want it?
- What will happen if she achieves her dream? The impact of success
- What will happen if she does NOT? The impact of failing and remaining stuck. Where will she be in the next 10 years of not changing?

As you ask the questions, this is your job:

- Listen silently without the uhs, and uhuh, and hmmms. Do not make sounds.
- After each question, ask her "anything else?"
- Take notes.
- Be fully present with her.

- Mirror her. Mirror whatever she said, and summarize it in the best way possible so she feels heard
- Ask the difficult questions like, What will your life look like in the next year two years five years 10 years if you do not make any change and if you stay this way and you continue to experience this pain in this worry? What will your life look like?
- Get into her world and help her to see the impact of not getting coaching.

Most people have become numb about their circumstances. They believe if you think positively and put on a happy face, their problems will disappear. So they never make a change. Your job is to help them find true happiness and freedom.

When your client gets the impact of her painful, excruciating her life, she will take action to change that.

Then you ask: "Do you want help with that? Do you want me to help you with that?"

This is the time to offer your programs. For example, I have a:

- 90 day transformational coaching program where we help you shed 20 pounds and become stronger and leaner
- I have this 90 day program that will help you restart your life
- I have this 90 day program where I help you get the job of your dreams

And give her the details of the program.

- The investment
- The time commitment
- The opportunity
- The results
- The delivery

For example:

"I have a wonderful program called "Get Engaged in a Year". It's a one-on-one program where we create a strategy for you to go from being single to getting engaged, and I am here with you in every single step during the process. We will meet once a week on Skype for 45 minutes and all the calls will be recorded for you. The investment is $4,000.00. You can pay in full or you can do the 4-pay option. What will work for you?"

Then you stay quiet and let her answer.

This is the fastest way that I have filled my client roster. My clients are fun, driven, they have the money, they love doing the home-work and they always pay on time.

In your journal, write down your first 90-day program. The name, the time commitment, the opportunity, the results, the delivery.

Do that now.

notes: ✍

Notes: ✍

CHAPTER 24

Being Grateful

Being grateful. Why would you want to be grateful? What's the benefit of being grateful, and what happens when you're not grateful? What happens when you get into the state of whining and complaining?

Why is it in your best interest to be grateful in your life. What are the benefits of gratefulness? How does being grateful effect your relationships, your business success, your health, your family life, your body, your community, your money, your bank account? You definitely want to know how being grateful can instantly change your life.

For the past few weeks, I have been immersed in a state of gratefulness, immersed in loving my life, and my sense of being, and my community, and my children, and what I'm about to create in this world.

I was looking at my life and at this year. Guess what happened? Yesterday happened. It's over. That's your life. Think about how old you are today, your yesterday is gone. You cannot have your yesterday again.

You can't have your life back. What you have now and today is the youngest you will ever be.

Life is going to happen.

Bankruptcy is going to happen, whether for you or someone you know. Divorce or relationship breakup, is going to happen, whether for you or someone you know. A health crisis is going to happen, to you or someone you know. Something unexpected is going to happen, that's life.

It may be money, relationships, health, or anything else. Things are going to happen, and when it happens, you will have to accept it.

The only way you can, as a believer is to accept things the way they come. If you lose one arm you say thank you, because you have one arm. If you lose two arms you say thank you, because you got two legs, Look at your eyelashes that you have, there are people that don't have eyelashes. I have a son with Cerebral Palsy, Spastic Quadriplegic, he uses a wheelchair. My son, Tarik, cannot get out of his wheelchair. He cannot get water or open the refrigerator, he can't do that.

You have legs, you can do that for yourself. There are people in this world who don't have anything. Our creator, has said, "When you are grateful, I will give you more to be grateful for", imagine that. If you are grateful, I will give you more to be grateful for. If you whine and complain, God will give you more to whine and complain about. If you think your life is bad now, wait to see what's coming. What's the benefit of whining and complaining?

In your journal, write down 10 things you are grateful for.

Do that now.

Notes: ✑

_____

_____

_____

_____

_____

_____

_____

Bonus Exercise

In your journal, write down 10 things you are grateful for every morning and every evening.

Gratefulness changes your energy system. Gratefulness changes the neuropath ways in your brain. Gratefulness is something that will shift your state and change your state from whining and complaining into gratefulness and when you're aligned and in the flow of gratefulness, The Creator sends amazing, crazy, audacious people and opportunities to your life.

Choose to be grateful. Make a choice to be grateful because stuff is going to happen in your life, but you can focus on saying, "Wow, I know this thing happened but you know what? I'm going to focus on what I have. I'm going to focus on what's working. I'm going to focus on all the amazing things in my life, the people in my life. I'm going to focus on what I'm going to create".

Since God woke you up today, you have an abundance of possibilities that you can create moving forward. Your past is behind you. Let's leave it there.

Notes:

CHAPTER 25

Facebook Lives

One of the best ways to grow your audience is Facebook live videos.

People have asked me how to create Facebook lives. How do I get amazing engagement? How do I get people to share my video with their list?

Here is my exact secret formula on how I actually do my Facebook lives.

- Find a great topic that your audience wants
- At the intro, immediately state what you will be speaking on. For example: "I'm going to teach you the three biggest mistakes women make when looking for a job, or the three biggest mistakes women make when they're going on a diet, or the three biggest mistakes women make when they're looking for looking for a spouse"
- Ask them to share
- Thank them for sharing
- Tell them you will be sharing too
- You or your team, share the video in all your groups and pages.
- Introduce myself again and welcome everyone to the video
- Mention your topic again and ask them if they have experienced anything like this or know anyone who has.
- Ask questions
- Wait for them to answer

- Give your audience answers that work!
- Answer their questions from the chat
- Ask them to subscribe so they never miss a video
- Create a contest
- Give stuff away

In your journal, write down when you will be doing your videos on Facebook. One of my clients did a 30-day blitz. One video a day. This positioned her as an expert and grew her page from 376 to 7,480 likes.

Do this now.

Notes: ✍

_____

_____

_____

_____

_____

_____

_____

_____

_____

_____

CHAPTER 26

Repurposing Content

Repurposing content is the best and easiest way to get your message out there without feeling overwhelmed.

This is what repurposing means. You write a bestselling book. You take content from that book and turn it into the following:

- Program
- Tweets
- Facebook posts
- Videos
- Talks
- Etc…

No need to reinvent the wheel. Do what the professionals do.

Here is the recipe I give to my private clients.

Every month, write one article. From that article, you have the content for that month.

- Daily Facebook statuses
- Facebook live videos (which will be uploaded on YouTube)
- Daily Tweets
- LinkedIn (post article)
- Create a talk
- Email marketing
- Instagram quotes

- Published white paper
- Submit to your local newspapers

In your journal now, write down the six articles that you will write for eh next six months.

Do this now.

Notes: ✍

CHAPTER 27

Publishing Your Book

So you want to write a book? Amazing! Best decision ever!

Here are the exact steps on how to write and publish a Kindle Amazon book.

First, you'll need an idea. Amazon is looking for a one problem, one solution book. This fits perfectly with your coaching ideas, your Facebook live videos, your Twitter tweets, your articles, and your lead magnet.

You already know who your client, and what problem she's having and what your solution is.

The book is set-up in a very simple way. My first bestseller was, "How to be a Muslim Woman, Divorced and Totally Confident". This book provided my ideal clients the solution they were looking for.

The format of the book was very simple: an introduction, conclusion, and how they can find you in the middle. You can have as many chapters as you want, as long as each one focuses on solving a problem for the client.

Once you have all of these ideas, you'll want to write down your chapter headings and all of the small points you want to make in each one.

Next, you'll need a voice recorder to record yourself speaking the book.

Next, you'll hire a transcriptionist to get your words transcribed.

Edited and proofreading is next.

Then, layout of your book.

Create a Kindle Amazon account so that you can set-up categories and add tags to your book.

At this point, if you haven't already contacted a graphic artist, you'll want to get that started.

This whole process will leave you with a Kindle version of your book ready to be uploaded and launched.

Have a launch event to encourage both friends and family to preview and buy your book.

Now that your Kindle book is finished, you can print a physical book.

Ta-da.

That was easy!

If you want us to help you with the book, now is the time to click the link on our **website.** All you have to do is let us know, and we will do everything we can to help you.

We are a one-stop shop - you can give us your manuscript and we will do the rest!

We will do a launch for you and guarantee that you'll be in Amazon's Top 10.

Once Amazon calls your book a best-seller, we can take that label and have it printed on the physical copies of your book.

Once you are a published, best-selling author, that title can never be taken away from you.

In your journal, write down the title of your book. Write down all of the chapter ideas you have so far.

Let's get started! Do that now.

Notes:

Notes: ✍

CHAPTER 28

Invitation

The more you practice, the more confidence you will have. Coaching is all about confidence and results, but it takes time and practice. Hiring a mentor is the best way that I have found to help. You don't want someone who is going to create a map for you, or is just pretending that they know what you need. You want someone who has been in the trenches, has experienced adversity, and has rebuilt her life into something extraordinary and phenomenal.

My mission is to empower and educate women, especially single moms and mothers who are struggling. Women who want to see their lives and families experience success. Women who want to see themselves as more than someone who gives birth or works in the kitchen. Women who have value and something to offer the world.

I am personally committed and passionate about helping women become financially free. Million Stars Academy, is the way that you can have everything you want and have all your dreams come true.

The modules are structured in a way that guarantees your success. It is a "no-fail system" that is basically "plug and play".

Million Stars Academy is a sisterhood, and a community where women are thriving. Women who hold each other up to a higher standard. This is the place for you!

There is no gossiping, no procrastination, no rejection, and no isolation. Here, you work as a team that hold each other up so that you can see your brilliance and beauty.

The team believes in you, even on the days where you wake up and don't feel like you believe in yourself. Those are the days when you especially need the team - your accountability partners.

Million Stars Academy ™ will help you create structures in your life that create a balance between health, family, love, intimacy, money, business, career, and charity. You will be connected spiritually to your Maker.

This is the place for you if you are ready to do something in this world and you know deep down inside that there is so much more you want to accomplish in life. Million Stars Academy ™ is a place for you if you want to be a part of the revolution and this game-changing academy of one million women all over the globe. Regardless of your race, religion, faith, ethnicity, background, culture, what your circumstances are, or what you've experienced in this world, we will help you add to the richness of your coaching world.

Million Stars Academy ™ can add success to your business.

At Million Stars Academy ™, we are looking for women who are ready to break through and give others a helping hand. A hand that will help change her life and change the world. I invite you to visit **MillionStarsMasterClass.com** and watch the incredible and content-rich training on Being A Coach.

If you're called to be a Million Stars Coach, go to **SpeakWithFatima.com** and book a time to speak with me or one of my certified coaches- right now.

We would love for you to be a part of the Million Stars Academy ™

We created a positive, inclusive environment where we help you, to step into your dreams and live your best life in both worlds. This is our motto, and we welcome you to join us right now!

CHAPTER 29

The Story Behind Million Stars

I have been through two divorces in my life. Million Stars Academy emerged as a result of those two very different, life-changing experiences.

During my first divorce, I left a multi-million dollar lifestyle with a home, cars, and lavish gardens. I was married to the richest, most influential Muslim family in Canada.

In June 2009, I took five children, from ages 4 to 19, and went into hiding. One of my children, Tarik, had cerebral palsy spastic quadriplegic. My new life started out in hiding, and I was diagnosed with adrenal burnout twice. I couldn't get out of bed, had no credit rating, no money, and no other family. My family was all in South Africa and I was receiving $535 in welfare. I really didn't know what to do and how I was going to feed my children.

I was fearful of everything: my future, my children's future, finding a home, being found, that my name would be disgraced and ruined, not doing the right thing, and that I was never going to get married again. Money was a very big fear because I didn't have any money. I was living with four children at home at one at the university, and Toronto was a challenging, expensive and tough place to live.

I could only imagine what other women went through, and sometimes I had the craziest thoughts. Maybe I could marry someone from overseas and charge money for the sponsorship. I was so depressed, I thought of suicide because, I didn't know where to turn. It was absolutely horrific. Everyone in my community had discarded me. My thyroid and adrenal condition was getting worse, and I needed prescription medication. It was one nightmare after another. I definitely got a chance to see what women go through when they want to leave an abusive relationship.

Fast forward to 2016. I had just celebrated my third anniversary with my second husband.

While I was on facebook, his girlfriend, a Christian Filipino woman who doesn't have any status in Canada, sent me pictures of them together.

She was the maid for his property management company, and since he had three or four jobs at one time, he was always on the road and was engaging in a five month affair with her.

I spoke to her, and validated the affair. I did not know what to expect because I had never been in a situation where my husband had cheated on me. The feeling of betrayal was so intense that I felt like I was having an emotional stroke.

I called him and asked him about it and he finally validated the story. I told him not to come home and that I would start the divorce proceedings right away. I couldn't stop crying. I had to shut down my business, and my kids and family tried to console me.

Something amazing happened out of this, though. This man had never provided for me financially and I was the sole provider. At this point, I had created a business with structures and a team. Even though, I was completely broken and devastated, my business still successfully continued.

Financially speaking, nothing in my life changed for me or my children.

Here I was, crying for 82 days, using essential oils, meditation, and prayer groups and I could not understand how this pain in my heart. At the same time, my business was still going strong. I did not have to deal with money issues, or a man threatening me, or threatening that he was not going to pay the bills because he never did. I had created a business that was independent of him. A business that would keep my children and I safe.

I could take the time to heal my heart, see doctors, join a prayer group, sleep when I wanted, and cry when I wanted, without fear.

I found myself asking my Creator what was the point of all this pain?

I finally got it.

Early in my life I had the experience of being a woman who had been through violence, trauma, abuse, and even discarded. In my second marriage, I had the experience of heartbreak and betrayal. Now that I have this experience, I can sit with a woman and with all honesty and authenticity say that I know what she's going through. I know her pain. I can now look back at both divorces and see how my and my children's lives have been changed.

The finances are intact, everything is mine, and the Creator made it so. I am more committed than ever to helping women become financially independent so you can have choices. If you are reading this book, and whether you stay or whether you leave, it must be your choice. You make the choice whether to get married or not. You make the choice whether to start your own business or not. You make the choice to immigrate to another country or stay. You make the choice to join the gym or have as many kids as you want.

It is a conscious choice that you make moment by moment and day by day. No one is forcing you to do anything. You get to step into your own power, brilliance, and authenticity.

I am giving you full permission to be the REAL YOU. That is how Million Stars Academy ™ was born, and I really hope you enjoy your journey with us.

Notes: ✍

CHAPTER 30

Limiting Beliefs

The human mind is naturally a wandering mind, and a wandering mind can turn into a negative mind, very easily.

Have you ever gotten in a car to drive somewhere and upon arrival, didn't even remember driving there? You might even wonder how in the world you got there! Did the car drive all by itself? Your subconscious mind did the driving for you because of the practice of mechanics - practicing the same habit over and over again. Your subconscious mind is running 90% of the programs, all the time.

Have you ever noticed that you promised you would never be like your parents in your relationships? Yet you found yourself in the same kind relationship like your parents had.

Maybe you decided to go on a diet program and your negative thoughts told you that you couldn't do it.

The good news is that this is normal! Even when you are doing good and happy things in your life, your mind will still wander to the negative. That's just how it works.

As you read this, you may have decided to open your own coaching business and make more money than you had before. Your subconscious mind will make you wonder what on earth is going on. The negative thoughts could engulf your thinking, if you allow it.

There are many different ways to overcome this, and, it will be your job to figure out what works best for you.

I've found the number one thing that works is focusing on my consciousness. Even when I'm driving my car and I stop at a red light, I use this time in a productive way. I sit there and focus. I say my prayers and affirmations of what I actually want to come in my life.

I use prayer and affirmations to reprogram my subconscious mind from negative habits of thinking into positive ones.

While you are waiting at the red light, you can think about how all these drivers on the road with you, are amazing, how you always get to places on time, and how your life is really working out so well for you.

In the beginning of this new habit, your mind will rebel. It's been practicing being negative for so long, it won't know what to do.

This will not seem natural to you. Even on the 2nd, 10th, or 20th time you say positive statements, it won't seem natural because it's a process, like learning a new language and a new way to speak.

It's a new habit that you are creating.

Let me give you an analogy of a cornfield and how this thinking would look. The first time attempt to walk through the corn field, there will be cornstalks in your way and you will have to move them with difficulty.

Every day you walk through the cornfield to get to the other side, it becomes a little easier as you step on the corn and make a small path.

One day, after a few weeks, you notice no more corn growing on the path that you take. And the more people use the path, the wider it becomes.

This is the same way your brain works! When you repeat affirmations over and over again, a neural pathway will be built in your brain. That pathway will become a road and that road will eventually become a superhighway.

That is what you want to create - a superhighway of positive thoughts and affirmations.

Don't be discouraged because this new thought process will still seem strange and new. You have to keep saying your positive thoughts and affirmations over and over again until you see all the wonderful results!

In your journal, write down 10 affirmations.

Do this now.

Notes: ✍

Notes: 🖎

CHAPTER 31

What is True Strength?

How do you define strength? What does strength mean to you?

The truth is, you never know how strong you are until something goes wrong in your life. If you say you have confidence, how did you know you had that confidence? Something had to happen in your life that enabled allowed you to discover that you are confident. Until that thing happened in your life, you didn't even know you were confident. And that's the interesting thing about trials and tribulations; it is the only time that you know how strong you are.

There is an analogy that I came upon which I found to be very interesting. When you are preparing a cup of tea, how do you know how strong the tea bag is? You don't know how strong it is until you put the teabag into hot water. The tea bag must go through the test of being placed in hot water in order to determine how strong it truly is. No matter how much you look at the tea bag or smell the leaves, the truth of the matter is, that it must be placed in hot water to see its true strength.

In the same way, you as a human being do not know your own strength until you get put into hot water. When we are placed in tough situations, that is when our true strength surfaces.

When you are placed in a situation that pulls your heart open and you are completely distraught, that's the time you know your true strength. You know because of your reactions. When you go through a breakdown and you feel completely lost because your heart is broken and your entire world has just fallen apart, it is in your reaction that you know your true strength. In that moment, in your reaction, in how you deal with that situation; that is when you discover what you are made of on the inside.

Now, if you hurt others, are you strong? If you take revenge on others, are you strong? If you become vengeful, are you strong? If you take away the rights of others, are you strong? If you become and ugly, are you strong? Are bullies, and perpetrators strong?

No, that is not strength -- that is called a weakness.

When something bad happens and you move away from God, that's a punishment. When terrible things are happening in your life and you have a trial and a tribulation and a difficulty and you go make a prayer and you put your hands up and you cry to God asking Him, "How can I fix this situation?"; that is the test.

God wants you to gain closeness to Him, especially in the toughest of times. He wants you to run back to Him. He wants his servant to run back to him. That's what He wants for you.

That is a cleansing for your soul and that is the time when you know your true strength. That is the time when you can hold firm to the rope of God because nobody else can help you overcome that situation except Him. That's when you know what true strength is; in your response, in your reaction to the pain, and in your reaction to the calamity.

When we think about it, life is very short and our time on this earth is finite. It is the end goal of paradise that we all seek to attain in the hereafter; a place of eternity. If our time in this world is short, why do we put so much emphasis on it instead of focusing on the prize to come? In the same way, why do we place so much emphasis on the small things in life? We get so caught up focusing all our energy towards the small things that we fail to see the bigger picture.

The only strength that is true strength is that which brings you closer to your Creator. That is the only strength that is true. Everything else is a make believe. Everything else is a fake.

Everything else is a mirage. Everything else was made up somewhere in your mind just like a fictional story.

So, how do you have a breakthrough and a transformation in the area of strength? Maybe you are looking at yourself thinking, "How do I change my world?"

What is something small that you can do to create true strength?

- First, you can pray. Prayers are the foundation of life.
- Another thing to do is really be focused on how you deal with others.
- Being conscious when life is NOT going the way you planned.
- Compete with others for good deeds.
- Start a club.
- Hold yourself and others accountable for reading scriptures (Holy Book), visiting the sick, giving charity, helping others.

Dedicate yourself in being a servant-leader, because that is where true strength lies!

In your journal, write down all the ways you can be a servant-leader.

Do that now.

Notes: ✍

_____

_____

_____

_____

_____

Notes:

Notes: ✍

Notes:

Notes: ✍

Notes:

Who is Fatima?

Who is Fatima Omar Khamissa? She was born in Johannesburg, South Africa and was the eldest of three siblings. Her parents were first-generation South Africans. Her grandparents on both sides of her family immigrated and left India with Gandhi to go to South Africa. While growing up in South Africa, she was taught Indian cultural beliefs and how to be a good girl. As the eldest of her siblings, she was very respectful, kind, and obedient.

She did exceptionally well in school and in her Islamic studies. Each year, she received the award for placing first or second in her class.

Her dad was a huge advocate for women's empowerment and education, and he knew that his daughters would never get a good education in apartheid South Africa.

In 1981, at the age of 14, Fatima left South Africa with her parents and siblings and arrived in Toronto, Canada. Prince Charles and Princess Diana were getting married that summer. It was an extremely dramatic change for her in the new schooling system and a brand new culture.

The first two years she spent getting accustomed to life in Canada and became a student who was always involved in many extracurricular activities. She was on the student council, and was voted as one who would be very successful in life. At the end of high school, Fatima was awarded a fully-paid four-year scholarship to McMaster University in Ontario.

Her father made a dramatic decision to return to South Africa with the family. Fatima's fate was locked in and she would give up the dream of going to McMaster University.

In Africa, she was accepted to a university but she hated every minute of it. She was unable to adjust to her new life in South Africa, which seemed like a strange place to her now.

She longed to return to Canada. A marriage proposal arrived from Canada, and she accepted.

In 1987, at the age of twenty, she married this man and returned to Canada. Unbeknownst to her, this man was a narcissist, also had bipolar disorder.

She was stuck. She chose to stay in that marriage, rather than bring shame to her parents. She had 5 children with this man and experienced 21 years and 11 months of violence.

She knew that her father-in-law was someone who truly loved her, so after he passed away, she took her 5 children and left that violent and abusive relationship and went into hiding in Toronto, Canada. Her life took a downward spiral from there when she was diagnosed with adrenal burnout, not once, but twice. She lost all her hair and nails and gained about 80 pounds. She was extremely emotional and depressed, and couldn't stop crying.

She didn't know how to make money, because she had never worked outside of the family business. She didn't have a credit rating, a credit card, a bank, or any family or friends that she could turn to.

She started her life over at this point, making videos, speaking, and teaching to women about what she had gone through in life. She was being vulnerable and courageous in sharing her story with the world.

Her volunteer work was being noticed. Awards arrived from The Government of Canada and The Government of Ontario.

She wrote a couple of books. She wanted to leave a legacy and make a difference in the world. She has written 5 books, and two of her books hit number one on Amazon in the same year!

She is a highly sought after international speaker. And her children are thriving.

With the help of her Creator, and the guidance of people and mentors around her, she has had quite an extraordinary life. She was unleashed and hit the ground running, and became an unstoppable force even through her illnesses.

She kept her children safe and turned her yearly income into a monthly income. Her calendar remains booked up for at least a year in advance and her clients absolutely love her!

She loves to experience success and loves to work with successful people. She created The Million Stars Academy Certification Program to fulfill on her dream so women globally do not have to suffer as she suffered.

Her dream is to empower, mentor and teach, one million women globally regardless of race, religion, faith, ethnicity, background, or history to become financially free.

She teaches women to have a viable coaching business so that they can make money and have an amazing business career. They can have choices and freedom to live the life that they want. She shares these ideas with you not to brag, but to simply show you what's possible.

If she could do it without family, money, or connections in a place where she had no friends or family, you can certainly do it too!

Fatima is a fighter! She fights for the rights of women and is a voice for the voiceless. Every day she stands up to give women more choices in their life. The Million Stars Academy ™, and all her other coaching programs, are designed to create independence and empowerment for women everywhere.

Fatima currently resides in Toronto, Canada with her four children. Her oldest is married, and lives with his wife near her. In her spare time she loves to travel, cook, and paint.

Made in the USA
Middletown, DE
29 April 2019